AF424140

Navigating the Caspian Sea: Its Strategic and Economic Importance

Copyright Page

TITLE: Navigating the Caspian Sea: Its Strategic and Economic Importance

1ST Edition

Copyright @ 2023

Roberto M. Rodriguez. All rights reserved.

ISBN: 9798223366201

Table of Contents

Navigating the Caspian Sea: Its Strategic and Economic Importance

By Roberto Miguel Rodriguez

Chapter 1: Introduction to the Caspian Sea

Overview of the Caspian Sea

The Caspian Sea, located between Europe and Asia, holds immense strategic and economic importance. With its vast reserves of oil and gas, the Caspian Sea has become a crucial region for exploration and production, attracting the attention of politicians, diplomats, and energy companies worldwide. This subchapter provides an overview of various aspects related to the Caspian Sea, highlighting its significance in different niches.

One of the key areas of interest in the Caspian Sea is oil and gas exploration. The region is recognized for its substantial hydrocarbon reserves and has become a major player in the global energy market. The subchapter explores the potential for further development and the challenges associated with extracting these resources.

Maritime security and geopolitics in the Caspian Sea region are also critical factors to consider. As the Caspian Sea borders several countries, including Russia, Iran, Azerbaijan, Kazakhstan, and Turkmenistan, the subchapter delves into the geopolitical dynamics and the importance of maintaining stability and security in the region.

Environmental sustainability and conservation efforts in the Caspian Sea are essential to preserve its delicate ecosystem. The subchapter highlights the ongoing initiatives to protect the sea's biodiversity and discusses the challenges faced by the countries surrounding it.

The Caspian Sea's role as a transportation hub and trade route is another aspect that cannot be overlooked. The subchapter explores the potential for improving transportation infrastructure and enhancing trade relations among the countries surrounding the sea.

Fisheries and aquaculture in the Caspian Sea are vital for the region's economy and food security. The subchapter discusses the challenges faced by the fishing industry and the need for sustainable practices to ensure the long-term viability of this resource.

Tourism and recreation opportunities in the Caspian Sea region are also emerging as a significant economic sector. The subchapter explores the potential for tourism development, highlighting the unique natural and cultural attractions of the area.

The Caspian Sea's renewable energy potential, such as wind and tidal power, is an area of growing interest. The subchapter explores the possibilities for harnessing these renewable resources and their contribution to the regional energy mix.

The Caspian Sea's strategic military and defense zone is also a topic of importance. The subchapter discusses the military significance of the sea and the implications for regional security.

Furthermore, the subchapter touches upon the cultural heritage and archaeological significance of the Caspian Sea, showcasing its rich history and archaeological sites.

Lastly, the subchapter explores the Caspian Sea as a source of rare minerals and resources, shedding light on the potential economic benefits associated with their extraction.

In conclusion, the Caspian Sea is a multifaceted region of immense strategic and economic importance. This subchapter provides a comprehensive overview of its significance in various niches, ranging from energy exploration to maritime security, environmental sustainability to cultural heritage, and fisheries to tourism. It aims to provide politicians, diplomats, and other interested parties with a holistic understanding of the Caspian Sea's importance and the opportunities and challenges it presents.

Historical significance of the Caspian Sea

The Caspian Sea holds immense historical significance that spans cultures, civilizations, and centuries. As we navigate the strategic and economic importance of this vast body of water, it is essential for politicians and diplomats to understand the historical context that has shaped its role in the region and the world.

The Caspian Sea has been a center of trade and commerce for thousands of years. Its strategic location at the crossroads of Europe and Asia has made it a vital transportation hub and trade route. Ancient civilizations such as the Persians and the Silk Road traders recognized its value and established thriving trade networks along its shores.

Throughout history, the Caspian Sea has also been a source of valuable resources. The region's abundant oil and gas reserves have played a significant role in shaping global energy markets. The exploration and production of these resources have attracted international investment and have been a driving force behind the economic development of the Caspian Sea region.

Beyond its economic importance, the Caspian Sea holds cultural heritage and archaeological significance. The ancient civilizations that flourished along its shores have left behind a rich tapestry of art, architecture, and artifacts. The study of these cultural remains provides insights into the history and development of the region.

Furthermore, the Caspian Sea serves as a strategic military and defense zone. Its proximity to conflict-prone areas has made it an area of interest for regional and global powers. Naval forces and military installations have been established to safeguard the region's security and protect its vital resources.

Environmental sustainability and conservation efforts are crucial to preserving the Caspian Sea's unique ecosystem. The sea is home to diverse marine life, including several endangered species. Concerted efforts are required to balance economic development with environmental conservation to ensure the long-term sustainability of the sea and its resources.

Tourism and recreation opportunities abound in the Caspian Sea region, attracting visitors from around the world. The sea's picturesque coastlines, pristine beaches, and recreational activities such as boating, fishing, and birdwatching make it a popular destination for both domestic and international tourists.

Lastly, the Caspian Sea holds promising potential as a source of renewable energy, such as wind and tidal power. As the world seeks to transition to clean and sustainable energy sources, the Caspian Sea's natural resources can contribute to this global effort.

In conclusion, understanding the historical significance of the Caspian Sea is vital for politicians and diplomats navigating its strategic and economic importance. From trade and resources to culture and defense, the Caspian Sea has played a central role in shaping the region and the world. It is our responsibility to ensure its sustainable development and preservation for future generations.

Geographical features and boundaries of the Caspian Sea

The Caspian Sea is the largest enclosed body of water on Earth, located between Europe and Asia. It is bordered by five countries: Russia to the northwest, Kazakhstan to the northeast, Turkmenistan to the southeast, Iran to the south, and Azerbaijan to the southwest. This subchapter explores the geographical features and boundaries of the Caspian Sea, providing valuable insights into the strategic and economic importance of this unique body of water.

The Caspian Sea spans an area of approximately 371,000 square kilometers, with a maximum depth of over 1,000 meters. It is a landlocked sea, which means it is not directly connected to any ocean. Instead, it is fed by several major rivers, including the Volga, Ural, and Kura, and has no outlet, resulting in a relatively high salt content.

Understanding the geographical features and boundaries of the Caspian Sea is crucial for politicians and diplomats, as well as those interested in its strategic and economic importance. The sea serves as a vital transportation hub and trade route, connecting the landlocked countries of Central Asia to global markets. It also holds vast reserves of oil and gas, making it a significant player in the energy sector.

Maritime security and geopolitics in the Caspian Sea region are of utmost importance, given the presence of valuable resources and the potential for territorial disputes. The determination of boundaries and the division of resources have been ongoing challenges, requiring diplomatic negotiations among the littoral states.

Environmental sustainability and conservation efforts in the Caspian Sea are essential for preserving the unique ecosystems and protecting the region's biodiversity. The sea is home to numerous fish species, making it a significant source of fisheries and aquaculture. Efforts to maintain sustainable practices are crucial for maintaining the ecological balance.

Furthermore, the Caspian Sea offers vast potential for renewable energy production, such as wind and tidal power. The development of these resources can contribute to the region's energy independence and reduce reliance on fossil fuels.

The Caspian Sea also holds significant cultural heritage and archaeological significance. Its shores are dotted with ancient sites and archaeological remains, shedding light on the region's rich history and cultural heritage.

Lastly, the Caspian Sea is a potential source of rare minerals and resources, providing opportunities for economic growth and development.

In conclusion, understanding the geographical features and boundaries of the Caspian Sea is vital for politicians, diplomats, and individuals interested in its strategic and economic importance. From oil and gas exploration to maritime security, environmental sustainability to cultural heritage, the Caspian Sea offers a multitude of opportunities and challenges that require careful consideration and cooperation among its littoral states.

Chapter 2: The Strategic and Economic Importance of the Caspian Sea

Political and economic significance of the Caspian Sea region

The Caspian Sea region holds immense political and economic significance, making it a topic of great interest for politicians and diplomats. This subchapter will explore the various aspects that contribute to the strategic and economic importance of the Caspian Sea, catering to the specific interests of our audience.

One of the key aspects of the Caspian Sea region is its rich oil and gas reserves. The region is home to significant oil and gas fields, attracting major international players in the energy sector. This has led to extensive exploration and production activities, making the Caspian Sea a vital source of energy for the global market. Understanding the dynamics of oil and gas exploration in the region is crucial for policymakers and diplomats involved in energy security and international negotiations.

Maritime security and geopolitics are also critical issues in the Caspian Sea region. The sea's strategic location, bordered by multiple countries, poses challenges related to territorial disputes, border control, and the fight against transnational crime. Diplomatic efforts to ensure stability and cooperation in the region are of utmost importance.

Environmental sustainability and conservation efforts in the Caspian Sea are vital for maintaining the ecological balance of this fragile ecosystem. Policymakers must address the growing concerns of pollution, overfishing, and habitat degradation to protect the region's biodiversity and safeguard its natural resources for future generations.

Moreover, the Caspian Sea serves as a crucial transportation hub and trade route, connecting Europe, Asia, and the Middle East.

Understanding the potential of this maritime route for trade and economic development is essential for diplomats and policymakers involved in regional cooperation and infrastructure development.

The Caspian Sea's fisheries and aquaculture industry provide a significant source of livelihood for the local communities. Policymakers need to support sustainable fishing practices and promote responsible aquaculture to ensure the long-term viability of this sector.

The region's tourism and recreation opportunities are yet to be fully explored, presenting immense potential for economic growth. Policymakers can tap into this potential by promoting sustainable tourism practices and developing infrastructure to attract visitors from around the world.

Furthermore, the Caspian Sea holds potential as a source of renewable energy, such as wind and tidal power. Policymakers should consider the development of these alternative energy sources to reduce dependence on fossil fuels and contribute to global efforts to combat climate change.

The Caspian Sea's strategic military and defense significance cannot be overlooked. Given the region's geopolitical complexities, policymakers and diplomats must navigate the delicate balance of military interests and cooperation to maintain stability and prevent conflicts.

Lastly, the Caspian Sea region boasts a rich cultural heritage and archaeological significance. Diplomats and policymakers should recognize the importance of preserving and promoting this heritage to foster cultural exchange, tourism, and regional cooperation.

In conclusion, the Caspian Sea region holds remarkable political and economic significance. Understanding the strategic and economic dimensions of the region is crucial for policymakers and diplomats involved in energy security, maritime security, trade, environmental sustainability, cultural preservation, and military defense. By navigating these facets effectively, we can ensure the region's stability, prosperity, and sustainable development.

Energy resources and reserves in the Caspian Sea

Energy resources and reserves in the Caspian Sea have emerged as a crucial topic in the geopolitics and strategic importance of the region. This subchapter explores the vast potential of the Caspian Sea as an energy hub, addressing the interests of politicians, diplomats, and various niches concerned with the strategic and economic importance of the sea.

The Caspian Sea region has long been recognized as a significant source of oil and gas reserves. With estimated oil reserves of over 48 billion barrels and gas reserves of around 8 trillion cubic meters, the Caspian Sea is a vital global energy supplier. This chapter delves into the exploration and production activities in the region, highlighting the major players, their investments, and the challenges they face.

Maritime security and geopolitics are essential aspects to consider in the Caspian Sea region. The unique geopolitical dynamics, involving five littoral countries, make the sea a focal point for diplomatic negotiations and strategic considerations. This chapter explores the complex relationships and potential conflicts arising from the competing interests of these nations.

While energy extraction is crucial, environmental sustainability and conservation efforts are equally important. The Caspian Sea is home to diverse ecosystems and unique species. This subchapter addresses the environmental challenges faced by the region and the ongoing efforts to protect and conserve its biodiversity.

The Caspian Sea's strategic location also positions it as a vital transportation hub and trade route. With increasing connectivity and infrastructure development, this chapter explores the potential for enhanced maritime trade and transportation in the region.

Beyond energy resources, the Caspian Sea offers opportunities for fisheries and aquaculture. Various species of fish and aquatic life thrive in its waters, making it an important source of livelihood for coastal communities. This chapter discusses the challenges and opportunities in the fishing industry.

The Caspian Sea's tourism and recreation potential is another important aspect to be explored. The region's rich cultural heritage, archaeological significance, and scenic beauty make it an attractive destination. This subchapter presents the various opportunities for tourism and recreation in the Caspian Sea region.

Furthermore, the Caspian Sea holds immense potential as a source of renewable energy, such as wind and tidal power. This chapter examines the prospects and challenges associated with harnessing these renewable resources to meet the growing energy demands of the region.

In addition to its economic significance, the Caspian Sea also serves as a strategic military and defense zone. This subchapter analyzes the military implications and security concerns in the region, including the presence of naval forces and the potential for conflicts.

Lastly, this chapter explores the Caspian Sea's role as a source of rare minerals and resources. The sea's unique geological composition offers opportunities for mining and extraction.

Overall, this subchapter provides a comprehensive overview of the energy resources and reserves in the Caspian Sea, addressing the interests of politicians, diplomats, and various niches concerned with the strategic and economic importance of the sea.

Trade routes and transportation networks in the Caspian Sea region

Trade routes and transportation networks in the Caspian Sea region have played a crucial role in shaping the strategic and economic importance of this vast body of water. For politicians and diplomats, understanding these trade routes and transportation networks is essential in harnessing the full potential of the Caspian Sea and promoting regional cooperation.

The Caspian Sea, with its abundant natural resources and strategic location, has emerged as a vital hub for trade and transportation. The sea's coastline spans multiple countries, including Russia, Iran, Azerbaijan, Kazakhstan, and Turkmenistan, making it a crossroads for various trade routes connecting Europe, Asia, and the Middle East.

One of the key trade routes in the Caspian Sea region is the North-South Transport Corridor, connecting India and the Persian Gulf with Russia and Northern Europe. This multimodal network of rail, road, and maritime routes offers a shorter and more efficient alternative to traditional shipping routes, reducing transportation costs and promoting economic integration.

Furthermore, the Caspian Sea serves as a vital transportation link for the region's oil and gas industry. Pipelines and shipping routes enable the transportation of energy resources from landlocked countries, such as Kazakhstan and Turkmenistan, to global markets. Developing and maintaining these transportation networks is crucial for the strategic and economic interests of both producing and consuming countries.

However, the Caspian Sea's trade routes and transportation networks also face challenges. Maritime security and geopolitical tensions in the region can disrupt the flow of goods and energy resources. Cooperation and dialogue among countries are essential to ensure the safety and security of these trade routes.

Environmental sustainability and conservation efforts are also critical in preserving the Caspian Sea's ecosystem and supporting the livelihoods of local communities. Balancing economic development with environmental protection is essential to ensure the long-term viability of the sea as a transportation hub and trade route.

In conclusion, trade routes and transportation networks in the Caspian Sea region are crucial for the strategic and economic interests of politicians and diplomats. Understanding and promoting these networks can unlock the full potential of the Caspian Sea, not only as a transportation hub but also as a source of renewable energy, a strategic military and defense zone, and a cultural and archaeological treasure. By addressing challenges and fostering regional cooperation, policymakers can harness the economic and geopolitical benefits of the Caspian Sea for the greater good of the region.

Chapter 3: Oil and Gas Exploration and Production in the Caspian Sea

Overview of oil and gas reserves in the Caspian Sea

The Caspian Sea, often referred to as the "Sea of Wealth," is home to vast reserves of oil and gas, making it a crucial region for the global energy market. In this subchapter, we will explore the strategic and economic importance of the Caspian Sea's oil and gas reserves, providing a comprehensive overview for politicians and diplomats.

The exploration and production of oil and gas in the Caspian Sea have been a driving force behind the region's economic growth and development. It is estimated that the sea holds approximately 48 billion barrels of oil and over 9 trillion cubic meters of natural gas, making it one of the largest hydrocarbon reserves in the world.

The Caspian Sea region has attracted significant international attention due to its potential to diversify global energy supplies and reduce dependence on traditional energy exporters. Countries bordering the Caspian Sea, such as Azerbaijan, Kazakhstan, and Turkmenistan, have become important players in the global energy market, attracting foreign investments and forging strategic partnerships with energy-consuming nations.

However, the exploration and production of oil and gas in the Caspian Sea present a unique set of challenges. Maritime security and geopolitics play a crucial role in shaping the region's energy landscape. The presence of multiple stakeholders, including Russia, Iran, and several Central Asian countries, has led to complex negotiations and disputes over the demarcation of maritime boundaries and the allocation of resources.

Furthermore, environmental sustainability and conservation efforts are paramount in the Caspian Sea region. Oil spills, pollution, and overfishing pose significant threats to the delicate ecosystem and biodiversity of the sea. Cooperation among the littoral states is essential to ensure responsible energy exploration and minimize the environmental impact.

The Caspian Sea's oil and gas reserves also contribute to its role as a transportation hub and trade route. The construction of pipelines, such as the Baku-Tbilisi-Ceyhan and the Trans-Caspian Gas Pipeline, have enhanced the region's connectivity and facilitated energy exports to Europe and beyond.

Additionally, the Caspian Sea holds untapped potential as a source of renewable energy, such as wind and tidal power. The exploitation of these resources can contribute to the transition to a more sustainable energy mix, reducing greenhouse gas emissions and addressing climate change concerns.

In conclusion, the Caspian Sea's oil and gas reserves have transformed the region into a vital player in the global energy market. Understanding the strategic and economic importance of these reserves is crucial for politicians and diplomats to navigate the complex dynamics of the Caspian Sea region effectively. However, it is equally important to ensure responsible energy exploration, preserve the environment, and foster cooperation among the littoral states to maximize the benefits of this invaluable resource.

Exploration and production activities in the Caspian Sea

The Caspian Sea, strategically located between Europe and Asia, plays a vital role in the global economy and security. This subchapter will delve into the exploration and production activities in the Caspian Sea, focusing on the oil and gas industry, its strategic and economic importance, as well as the challenges and opportunities it presents.

The Caspian Sea region is known for its vast oil and gas reserves, making it a significant player in the global energy market. Politicians and diplomats must be aware of the potential implications of these reserves, as they can greatly influence both regional and global energy security. Understanding the dynamics of oil and gas exploration and production in the Caspian Sea is crucial for effective policymaking.

Maritime security and geopolitics are also of utmost importance in the Caspian Sea region. The exploration and production activities attract international attention and create a complex web of interests among the littoral states and external stakeholders. Addressing these security concerns and establishing cooperative frameworks is vital for maintaining stability and ensuring the uninterrupted flow of energy resources.

Furthermore, environmental sustainability and conservation efforts in the Caspian Sea are essential for maintaining the ecological balance of this unique ecosystem. The exploration and production activities must be conducted with strict adherence to environmental regulations to prevent any adverse impacts on marine life and habitats.

The Caspian Sea's potential as a transportation hub and trade route is another significant aspect to consider. The development of port infrastructure and the enhancement of maritime connectivity can unlock new trade opportunities and boost economic growth in the region. Political leaders and diplomats must explore ways to leverage the Caspian Sea's strategic location to foster regional cooperation and economic integration.

Additionally, the Caspian Sea offers immense potential as a source of renewable energy, such as wind and tidal power. Policymakers should explore and support initiatives that harness these resources, promoting a sustainable and diversified energy mix.

The Caspian Sea's strategic military and defense zone should also be a topic of concern. Developing effective security mechanisms and cooperation among littoral states can contribute to regional stability and deter any potential threats.

The cultural heritage and archaeological significance of the Caspian Sea further enrich its value. Preserving and promoting these aspects can contribute to tourism and recreation opportunities, attracting visitors from around the world and fostering cultural exchange.

Lastly, the Caspian Sea's potential as a source of rare minerals and resources should not be overlooked. Diplomats should explore avenues for responsible and sustainable extraction, ensuring that these resources benefit the region's development without causing harm to the environment or local communities.

In conclusion, understanding the exploration and production activities in the Caspian Sea is vital for politicians and diplomats. The strategic and economic importance, maritime security, environmental sustainability, and various opportunities it presents require careful consideration and collaboration among all stakeholders. By navigating the complexities of the Caspian Sea, policymakers can unlock its full potential and foster regional cooperation and prosperity.

Challenges and opportunities in the oil and gas sector

The oil and gas sector plays a crucial role in the strategic and economic importance of the Caspian Sea region. This subchapter aims to highlight the challenges and opportunities faced by the sector and provide insights for politicians and diplomats.

One of the major challenges in the oil and gas sector is the complex geopolitics and maritime security in the Caspian Sea region. With multiple countries sharing the sea, disputes over territorial boundaries and exclusive rights have emerged. These political conflicts can hinder the exploration and production of oil and gas reserves, making it essential for politicians and diplomats to engage in diplomatic negotiations and foster cooperation among the neighboring countries.

Furthermore, environmental sustainability and conservation efforts are paramount in the Caspian Sea region. The extraction and transportation of oil and gas can pose significant risks to the delicate ecosystem. Therefore, there is a need for stringent regulations and sustainable practices to mitigate the environmental impact of the sector. Policymakers should focus on promoting the use of advanced technologies and supporting research and development initiatives to reduce the ecological footprint.

Despite these challenges, the oil and gas sector in the Caspian Sea region presents immense opportunities. The vast reserves of oil and gas in the region can contribute to energy security and economic growth. By leveraging these resources, countries can attract foreign investments, create job opportunities, and enhance their geopolitical influence. Moreover, the Caspian Sea can also serve as a transportation hub and trade route, connecting Europe, Asia, and the Middle East. This offers the potential for increased regional integration and trade cooperation.

Additionally, the Caspian Sea holds promise as a source of renewable energy, such as wind and tidal power. Investing in these green technologies can promote a sustainable energy transition and reduce dependence on fossil fuels. Furthermore, the region's rich cultural heritage and archaeological significance can be leveraged to develop tourism and recreation opportunities, boosting the local economies.

In conclusion, the oil and gas sector in the Caspian Sea region faces numerous challenges related to geopolitics, maritime security, and environmental sustainability. However, by addressing these challenges and seizing the opportunities, politicians and diplomats can foster regional cooperation, promote sustainable practices, and harness the economic potential of the sector. It is crucial for policymakers to prioritize dialogue and collaboration to ensure a prosperous and resilient future for the Caspian Sea region.

Chapter 4: Maritime Security and Geopolitics in the Caspian Sea Region

Geopolitical dynamics in the Caspian Sea region

The Caspian Sea region is a unique area that holds significant strategic and economic importance, making it a focal point for politicians and diplomats. This subchapter will delve into the geopolitical dynamics that shape the region, shedding light on its complexities and implications for various niches.

In recent years, the Caspian Sea has emerged as a critical player in global energy markets. Its vast oil and gas reserves have attracted the attention of major international players, leading to increased exploration and production activities. As such, understanding the strategic and economic importance of the Caspian Sea in terms of energy resources is crucial for policymakers and diplomats.

Additionally, the maritime security and geopolitical situation in the Caspian Sea region cannot be overlooked. With multiple countries sharing its coastline, including Russia, Iran, Kazakhstan, Turkmenistan, and Azerbaijan, tensions and disputes over territorial claims and resource exploitation have arisen. Navigating these challenges and ensuring stability in the region is a priority for politicians and diplomats.

Environmental sustainability and conservation efforts are also paramount in the Caspian Sea region. The delicate ecosystem and unique biodiversity of the sea require protection to preserve its natural resources. Policymakers and diplomats must collaborate on initiatives aimed at sustainable development and conservation practices to safeguard the Caspian Sea for future generations.

Furthermore, the Caspian Sea's potential as a transportation hub and trade route is noteworthy. Its geographic location connects Central Asia, the Caucasus, and Europe, making it an ideal transit route for goods and commodities. Enhancing transportation infrastructure and promoting trade cooperation will provide economic opportunities and foster regional integration.

Other aspects that deserve attention include fisheries and aquaculture, tourism and recreation opportunities, renewable energy sources, military and defense strategies, cultural heritage, and archaeological significance, as well as the potential for rare minerals and resources. These niches contribute to the overall understanding of the Caspian Sea region's geopolitical dynamics and offer avenues for collaboration and cooperation between nations.

In conclusion, the geopolitical dynamics in the Caspian Sea region are multifaceted and require the attention of politicians and diplomats. Understanding the strategic and economic importance, addressing maritime security concerns, promoting environmental sustainability, and exploring opportunities in various niches are crucial for effective governance and regional cooperation. By navigating these dynamics, stakeholders can harness the potential of the Caspian Sea for the benefit of all involved.

Maritime security challenges and threats in the Caspian Sea

Introduction:

The Caspian Sea, surrounded by five countries, plays a crucial role in various sectors, including energy, trade, environment, and culture. However, the sea also faces several maritime security challenges and threats that require the attention of politicians and diplomats. This subchapter aims to shed light on these issues and propose possible solutions.

Piracy and Maritime Crime:

The Caspian Sea is not immune to piracy and maritime crime, which pose significant threats to the safety and security of vessels and crews. These criminal activities disrupt trade and investment, affecting the region's economic stability. Politicians and diplomats must collaborate to establish a comprehensive maritime security framework to combat piracy effectively, enforce laws, and enhance cooperation among the littoral states.

Illegal Fishing and Overfishing:

The Caspian Sea's rich biodiversity, particularly its fish stocks, is under threat due to illegal fishing and overfishing. These activities deplete resources, disrupt the ecosystem, and harm local communities that rely on fishing for their livelihoods. Policymakers and diplomats should prioritize the implementation of sustainable fishing practices, strengthen surveillance, and enhance cooperation to combat illegal fishing and promote responsible fishing activities.

Territorial Disputes:

The Caspian Sea region is known for its complex territorial disputes among the littoral states. These disputes, primarily related to boundary delimitation and the division of resources, can escalate into conflicts, jeopardizing the stability of the region. Politicians and diplomats must engage in constructive dialogues, negotiate fair agreements, and establish mechanisms to resolve these disputes peacefully, ensuring the equitable distribution of resources and fostering regional cooperation.

Terrorism and Transnational Threats:

The Caspian Sea region is not immune to transnational threats, including terrorism, smuggling, and drug trafficking. These activities undermine security, stability, and economic development. Policymakers and diplomats should strengthen intelligence sharing, border control measures, and regional cooperation to combat these threats effectively. Additionally, addressing the root causes of extremism, promoting socio-economic development, and enhancing cultural exchanges can contribute to long-term stability and security in the region.

Conclusion:

Addressing maritime security challenges and threats in the Caspian Sea requires the collective efforts of politicians and diplomats. By focusing on issues such as piracy, illegal fishing, territorial disputes, and transnational threats, policymakers can ensure the safety and security of the region. Moreover, fostering regional cooperation, dialogue, and sustainable practices will not only protect the Caspian Sea's strategic and economic importance but also contribute to its environmental sustainability and preserve its cultural heritage for future generations.

Cooperation and conflict resolution efforts in the region

In the complex and strategically important region of the Caspian Sea, cooperation and conflict resolution efforts have played a crucial role in maintaining stability and fostering economic growth. With a diverse range of interests at stake, including oil and gas exploration, maritime security, environmental sustainability, and cultural heritage, politicians and diplomats have been actively engaged in finding common ground and resolving conflicts.

One of the key areas where cooperation has been essential is in oil and gas exploration and production. The Caspian Sea is rich in hydrocarbon reserves, and countries in the region have been working together to develop these resources in a mutually beneficial manner. Through negotiations and agreements, they have resolved disputes over territorial boundaries and sharing of resources, paving the way for joint ventures and investment opportunities. This cooperation has not only boosted economic growth but also enhanced regional stability by reducing the potential for conflicts over energy resources.

Another critical area where cooperation is crucial is maritime security and geopolitics. Given the Caspian Sea's geopolitical significance and its proximity to conflict-prone regions, ensuring the safety and security of maritime routes is of utmost importance. Politicians and diplomats have been actively engaged in discussions to establish mechanisms for cooperation in maritime security, including joint patrols, information sharing, and capacity building. By working together, they have succeeded in combating piracy, smuggling, and other security threats, thereby fostering stability and promoting economic activities in the region.

Environmental sustainability and conservation efforts are also high on the agenda for politicians and diplomats. The Caspian Sea is home to diverse marine ecosystems and wildlife, and preserving its ecological balance is essential for the long-term well-being of the region. Through collaborative efforts, countries in the region have established conservation programs, enacted legislation to protect the environment, and implemented sustainable fishing practices. These initiatives not only safeguard the region's natural resources but also promote eco-tourism and recreational opportunities, contributing to economic growth and job creation.

In conclusion, cooperation and conflict resolution efforts in the Caspian Sea region have played a vital role in maintaining stability, fostering economic growth, and addressing various challenges. Through negotiations and agreements, politicians and diplomats have successfully resolved disputes, promoted joint ventures, and implemented measures for maritime security, environmental conservation, and sustainable development. By continuing to work together, they can ensure the region's long-term prosperity and overcome future challenges.

Chapter 5: Environmental Sustainability and Conservation Efforts in the Caspian Sea

Environmental issues and challenges in the Caspian Sea

The Caspian Sea, a unique and valuable natural resource, faces numerous environmental issues and challenges that require urgent attention from politicians and diplomats. As the largest enclosed body of water in the world, the Caspian Sea plays a vital role in the strategic and economic interests of the region. However, the sea's fragile ecosystem is under threat, demanding immediate action to ensure its sustainability and conservation.

One of the most pressing concerns is the impact of oil and gas exploration and production in the Caspian Sea. The extraction and transportation of these resources have led to oil spills and pollution, endangering marine life and disrupting the delicate balance of the ecosystem. It is imperative for policymakers and diplomats to prioritize sustainable practices and stricter regulations in the oil and gas sector to minimize the negative environmental consequences.

Maritime security and geopolitics also pose significant challenges to the Caspian Sea region. Disputes over territorial boundaries and conflicting interests among the littoral states can hinder effective environmental management. Cooperation and dialogue between nations are crucial to establish a comprehensive framework that addresses environmental concerns while maintaining security and stability in the region.

Conservation efforts in the Caspian Sea must be a top priority. The unique biodiversity and fragile ecosystems, including wetlands and fisheries, require protection and restoration. Sustainable fishing practices, the establishment of marine protected areas, and the promotion of biodiversity conservation are essential to preserve the natural heritage of the Caspian Sea.

Furthermore, the Caspian Sea's potential as a transportation hub and trade route must be balanced with environmental considerations. The construction of ports, shipping lanes, and pipelines should be carefully planned and executed, taking into account the potential impact on marine life and water quality.

In addition to traditional energy sources, the Caspian Sea holds great potential as a source of renewable energy, such as wind and tidal power. Policymakers and diplomats should explore opportunities to harness these clean energy sources while minimizing the ecological footprint.

The Caspian Sea also holds cultural heritage and archaeological significance, adding to its value as a natural resource. Preservation and promotion of these cultural assets should be integrated into environmental conservation efforts, creating a holistic approach that protects both the natural and cultural heritage of the region.

Lastly, the Caspian Sea's vast mineral and resource deposits offer economic opportunities, but their extraction must be conducted in an environmentally responsible manner. Sustainable mining practices and proper waste management are essential to prevent long-term damage to the ecosystem.

In conclusion, addressing the environmental issues and challenges in the Caspian Sea requires the collective efforts of politicians and diplomats. By prioritizing sustainable practices, promoting conservation efforts, and balancing economic interests with environmental considerations, the Caspian Sea can be safeguarded for future generations, ensuring its strategic and economic importance while preserving its natural beauty.

Conservation initiatives and sustainable practices

In recent years, the Caspian Sea region has witnessed an increasing focus on conservation initiatives and sustainable practices. As the strategic and economic importance of the sea continues to grow, it is crucial for politicians and diplomats to prioritize environmental sustainability and conservation efforts in their policies and decision-making processes.

The Caspian Sea is not only a vital source of oil and gas exploration and production but also a hub for transportation and trade routes. As such, it is imperative to ensure that these activities are carried out with the utmost regard for environmental conservation. Several initiatives have been implemented to minimize the impact of these industries on the Caspian Sea's delicate ecosystem. These include the adoption of advanced technologies to reduce carbon emissions and the implementation of strict regulations to prevent oil spills and other environmental disasters.

Maritime security and geopolitics in the Caspian Sea region are also closely linked to conservation efforts. The stability and security of the region are essential for the sustainable management of the sea's resources. Cooperation among countries is crucial in combating illegal fishing, piracy, and other maritime threats that not only harm the environment but also jeopardize the economic potential of the Caspian Sea.

Furthermore, the Caspian Sea holds significant potential as a source of renewable energy, such as wind and tidal power. By investing in these sustainable energy sources, countries in the region can reduce their reliance on fossil fuels and contribute to global efforts to combat climate change.

The Caspian Sea's rich biodiversity also presents opportunities for sustainable fisheries and aquaculture practices. By implementing responsible fishing practices, such as setting catch limits and protecting spawning grounds, politicians and diplomats can ensure the long-term viability of the fishing industry while preserving the Caspian Sea's unique ecosystem.

In addition to its economic and strategic significance, the Caspian Sea region offers vast potential for tourism and recreation. By promoting sustainable tourism practices, such as responsible waste management and the protection of natural habitats, politicians and diplomats can attract visitors while preserving the region's natural beauty for future generations.

Lastly, the Caspian Sea's cultural heritage and archaeological significance should not be overlooked. Efforts should be made to preserve and protect these valuable archaeological sites, as they provide insights into the region's history and contribute to its cultural identity.

In conclusion, conservation initiatives and sustainable practices are fundamental to the responsible management of the Caspian Sea region. By prioritizing environmental sustainability, politicians and diplomats can ensure the long-term economic and strategic importance of the sea while preserving its natural resources, supporting local communities, and protecting its unique ecosystem for future generations.

International cooperation for environmental protection

International cooperation for environmental protection is of utmost importance in the Caspian Sea region, as it is a unique and fragile ecosystem that requires concerted efforts from all nations involved. With its strategic and economic significance, the Caspian Sea attracts politicians and diplomats from various countries who must understand the need for environmental sustainability and conservation efforts in this region.

The Caspian Sea is not only rich in oil and gas reserves but also home to diverse marine life and habitats. Therefore, it is crucial to establish international cooperation to protect and preserve this delicate ecosystem. Collaborative efforts such as sharing scientific research, implementing joint conservation projects, and creating transnational agreements are key to ensuring the long-term sustainability of the Caspian Sea.

One of the major concerns in the Caspian Sea region is the impact of oil and gas exploration and production on the environment. International cooperation can play a significant role in setting and enforcing strict environmental regulations for offshore drilling, pipeline construction, and waste disposal. By working together, politicians and diplomats can ensure that these activities are carried out in an environmentally responsible manner, minimizing the negative impact on the ecosystem.

Maritime security and geopolitics in the Caspian Sea region are closely linked to environmental protection. A stable and secure region is essential for effective environmental conservation. Therefore, it is vital for politicians and diplomats to engage in dialogue and cooperation to address security challenges and find mutually beneficial solutions that promote both security and environmental sustainability.

Furthermore, the Caspian Sea has the potential to become a transportation hub and trade route, providing economic opportunities for the region. However, it is crucial to develop sustainable transport infrastructure and practices to minimize the environmental impact. International cooperation can facilitate the exchange of best practices and the implementation of environmentally friendly technologies, ensuring that the Caspian Sea remains a viable and sustainable trade route.

In conclusion, international cooperation for environmental protection is essential in the Caspian Sea region. Politicians and diplomats must recognize the strategic and economic importance of the sea while also understanding the need for environmental sustainability and conservation efforts. Through collaborative efforts, it is possible to protect the fragile ecosystem of the Caspian Sea, ensuring its long-term viability for future generations.

Chapter 6: Caspian Sea as a Transportation Hub and Trade Route

Importance of the Caspian Sea for regional and international trade

The Caspian Sea has long been recognized as a crucial hub for regional and international trade, playing a vital role in connecting various countries and facilitating economic activities. Its strategic location and vast resources make it a significant area of interest for politicians, diplomats, and a wide range of niche sectors.

The Caspian Sea is a key player in the global oil and gas industry, with substantial reserves and production capabilities. It holds immense potential for energy exploration and production, attracting investors and businesses from around the world. The sea's resources provide an opportunity for countries in the region to strengthen their economies, develop infrastructure, and enhance their energy security.

Maritime security and geopolitics in the Caspian Sea region are essential considerations for politicians and diplomats. The sea's strategic location and its proximity to major global powers make it a significant geopolitical hotspot. Cooperation among countries bordering the Caspian Sea is crucial for ensuring stability, resolving disputes, and safeguarding regional peace.

Environmental sustainability and conservation efforts in the Caspian Sea are of utmost importance. The sea's unique ecosystem, diverse marine life, and fragile environment need protection to maintain its ecological balance. Collaboration among nations is vital in implementing conservation measures, such as controlling pollution, preserving habitats, and promoting sustainable fishing practices.

The Caspian Sea serves as a crucial transportation hub and trade route, connecting Central Asia, the Caucasus, and Europe. Its navigable waters allow for the movement of goods, fostering regional integration and economic growth. Developing efficient transport infrastructure and improving logistics networks will enhance trade opportunities and facilitate economic cooperation.

Fisheries and aquaculture in the Caspian Sea contribute significantly to the region's food security and economic development. The sea is home to various commercially valuable fish species, making it a vital resource for the fishing industry. Sustainable management practices and international cooperation are necessary to ensure the long-term viability of the Caspian Sea's fisheries.

The Caspian Sea region offers immense potential for tourism and recreation, attracting visitors with its natural beauty, historical sites, and cultural heritage. Developing sustainable tourism infrastructure and promoting responsible tourism practices will not only boost local economies but also raise awareness about the importance of preserving the Caspian Sea's natural and cultural assets.

Furthermore, the Caspian Sea's renewable energy potential, such as wind and tidal power, presents a significant opportunity for countries in the region to diversify their energy sources. Investing in renewable energy technologies can reduce dependence on fossil fuels, mitigate climate change, and foster sustainable development.

The Caspian Sea's strategic military and defense zone status cannot be overlooked. Its location and geopolitical significance make it a crucial area for military presence and operations. Cooperation among nations, clear boundaries, and effective security mechanisms are essential for maintaining stability and preventing conflicts.

The Caspian Sea also holds cultural heritage and archaeological significance, with numerous ancient civilizations having thrived along its shores. Exploring and preserving this rich history not only promotes cultural exchange but also enhances the region's tourism potential.

Lastly, the Caspian Sea is a valuable source of rare minerals and resources. The exploration and extraction of these resources offer economic opportunities and can contribute to the development of industries in the region.

In conclusion, the Caspian Sea's importance for regional and international trade cannot be overstated. Its energy resources, strategic location, transportation capabilities, environmental significance, and cultural heritage make it a multifaceted and crucial area of interest for politicians, diplomats, and various niche sectors. Cooperation, sustainable practices, and responsible management are key to harnessing the full potential of the Caspian Sea while preserving its natural and cultural assets for future generations.

Infrastructure development and connectivity projects

Infrastructure development and connectivity projects are crucial for unlocking the full potential of the Caspian Sea region. As politicians and diplomats, it is essential to understand the strategic and economic importance of these projects and their impact on various niches within the region.

One of the significant aspects of infrastructure development in the Caspian Sea region is the establishment of transportation hubs and trade routes. Improved connectivity through roads, railways, and ports can enhance regional integration and facilitate the movement of goods and people. This, in turn, can boost trade, attract investments, and create economic opportunities for the countries surrounding the Caspian Sea.

Furthermore, the development of infrastructure can contribute to the growth of the oil and gas industry in the region. As exploration and production activities continue to expand, the need for efficient transportation infrastructure becomes paramount. Building pipelines and other logistical facilities can ensure the smooth flow of energy resources and enhance energy security for both exporting and importing countries.

In addition to energy infrastructure, the Caspian Sea can also serve as a source of renewable energy. The region has tremendous potential for harnessing wind and tidal power, which can contribute to diversifying the energy mix and reducing reliance on fossil fuels. By investing in renewable energy projects, the Caspian Sea countries can promote environmental sustainability and contribute to global efforts to combat climate change.

Infrastructure development in the Caspian Sea region is not only limited to energy and transportation but also includes the improvement of maritime security and defense capabilities. The strategic location of the Caspian Sea makes it crucial for ensuring regional stability and safeguarding critical maritime routes. Strengthening military and defense infrastructure can deter potential threats and enhance the security of the region.

Moreover, infrastructure projects can also support the preservation of cultural heritage and archaeological significance of the Caspian Sea. By investing in the restoration and conservation of historical sites, the countries can promote tourism and recreation opportunities. This, in turn, can boost the local economy and create employment opportunities for the local population.

Lastly, infrastructure development can also tap into the Caspian Sea's potential as a source of rare minerals and resources. By investing in mining and extraction facilities, the countries can explore the untapped mineral wealth and promote economic growth.

In conclusion, infrastructure development and connectivity projects play a vital role in unlocking the strategic and economic potential of the Caspian Sea region. By focusing on transportation hubs, renewable energy, maritime security, cultural heritage, and resource extraction, the countries can foster regional integration, attract investments, and ensure sustainable development for the benefit of all stakeholders. As politicians and diplomats, it is crucial to prioritize and support these projects to promote stability, prosperity, and cooperation in the Caspian Sea region.

Opportunities and challenges for enhancing transportation networks

Transportation networks play a pivotal role in the development and progress of any region. In the case of the Caspian Sea, enhancing transportation networks presents both opportunities and challenges that need to be carefully addressed. This subchapter explores the various aspects related to the transportation hub and trade route potential of the Caspian Sea, considering its strategic and economic importance, as well as the interests of politicians and diplomats.

The Caspian Sea region is rich in natural resources, particularly oil and gas, making it a vital player in the global energy market. The development of transportation networks can significantly boost the export potential of these resources, creating opportunities for economic growth and prosperity. Politicians and diplomats have a crucial role in fostering cooperation among the Caspian Sea littoral states to facilitate the transportation of these valuable commodities.

However, enhancing transportation networks in the Caspian Sea region also poses challenges that need to be addressed. Maritime security and geopolitics are major concerns, as any disruption to transportation routes can have severe consequences for regional stability and global energy markets. Therefore, politicians and diplomats must work together to establish robust security mechanisms to safeguard these vital sea lanes.

Furthermore, environmental sustainability and conservation efforts must be at the forefront of any transportation network enhancement plans. The Caspian Sea is home to diverse marine life, and any infrastructure development should be conducted with utmost care to minimize ecological damage. Politicians and diplomats need to prioritize environmental protection, ensuring that transportation networks do not compromise the delicate balance of the Caspian Sea ecosystem.

The Caspian Sea also holds immense potential as a source of renewable energy, such as wind and tidal power. The development of transportation networks can facilitate the harnessing of these resources, contributing to a sustainable energy future. Politicians and diplomats should explore opportunities for collaboration in renewable energy projects, promoting the Caspian Sea as a hub for clean energy production.

Furthermore, the transportation hub and trade route potential of the Caspian Sea can boost other sectors such as fisheries, aquaculture, tourism, and recreation. Politicians and diplomats should work towards creating favorable conditions for the growth of these industries, highlighting the economic benefits they can bring to the region.

In conclusion, enhancing transportation networks in the Caspian Sea region presents numerous opportunities for economic growth and development. However, it also poses challenges related to maritime security, environmental sustainability, and geopolitical tensions. Politicians and diplomats have a crucial role to play in addressing these challenges and capitalizing on the opportunities, ensuring the strategic and economic importance of the Caspian Sea is maximized for the benefit of all stakeholders.

Chapter 7: Fisheries and Aquaculture in the Caspian Sea

Biodiversity and fishery resources in the Caspian Sea

The Caspian Sea, nestled between Europe and Asia, is not only the largest enclosed body of water on Earth but also an ecological treasure trove. Its unique combination of freshwater and saltwater, along with its diverse ecosystems, makes it a haven for biodiversity and fishery resources. This subchapter explores the significance of these resources and their implications for the region's strategic and economic interests.

The Caspian Sea boasts an astonishing array of biodiversity, with over 400 different species of fish and numerous other marine organisms. This diversity is attributed to the sea's distinct water chemistry, which supports a wide range of habitats. Politicians and diplomats must recognize the importance of protecting and preserving this biodiversity to maintain the ecological balance and sustain the fishery resources.

Fishery resources in the Caspian Sea have long been a vital source of income and sustenance for the countries surrounding its shores. The sea's rich fish stocks, including sturgeon, herring, and trout, are highly valued for their commercial and cultural significance. However, overfishing and habitat destruction have posed significant threats to the sustainability of these resources.

Addressing these challenges requires strategic and collaborative efforts among the Caspian Sea nations. Politicians and diplomats play a crucial role in promoting responsible fishing practices, establishing conservation measures, and implementing sustainable aquaculture methods. These actions not only ensure the long-term viability of fishery resources but also contribute to the socioeconomic development of the region.

Furthermore, the preservation of biodiversity and fishery resources in the Caspian Sea has broader implications beyond environmental concerns. The availability of abundant fish stocks can enhance the food security of the region, reducing dependence on external sources. It also presents economic opportunities through the export of fish and fish products, stimulating trade and generating revenue.

By recognizing the strategic and economic importance of the Caspian Sea's biodiversity and fishery resources, politicians and diplomats can advocate for policies that prioritize conservation and sustainability. This commitment will not only safeguard the ecological integrity of the region but also ensure its long-term prosperity. Through international cooperation and responsible management, the Caspian Sea can continue to thrive as a vital resource for both the present and future generations.

Aquaculture practices and sustainable fishery management

Aquaculture practices and sustainable fishery management are of vital importance in the Caspian Sea region, considering its strategic and economic significance. As politicians and diplomats, it is crucial to understand the role of aquaculture and sustainable fishery management in maintaining the balance of this unique ecosystem and ensuring the long-term prosperity of the region.

The Caspian Sea is home to a diverse range of fish species, including sturgeon, which is highly valued for its caviar. However, overfishing and illegal fishing practices have led to a decline in fish populations, threatening the delicate balance of the ecosystem and the livelihoods of local communities dependent on fishing.

To address these challenges, sustainable fishery management practices must be implemented. This includes setting catch limits, regulating fishing gear, and establishing protected areas to allow fish populations to recover. Additionally, the promotion of aquaculture can help reduce pressure on wild fish stocks by providing an alternative source of seafood production.

Aquaculture, or fish farming, involves the cultivation of fish and other aquatic organisms in controlled environments. This practice not only provides a sustainable source of seafood but also offers economic opportunities for local communities. By promoting responsible aquaculture practices, policymakers can enhance food security, create jobs, and boost economic growth in the region.

Furthermore, sustainable fishery management and aquaculture practices contribute to the environmental sustainability and conservation efforts in the Caspian Sea. By protecting fish populations and their habitats, we can ensure the preservation of biodiversity and safeguard the Caspian Sea's fragile ecosystem for future generations.

In conclusion, aquaculture practices and sustainable fishery management play a vital role in the strategic and economic importance of the Caspian Sea. By implementing responsible fishing practices and promoting aquaculture, we can ensure the long-term sustainability of fish stocks, support local communities, and preserve the Caspian Sea's unique ecosystem. As politicians and diplomats, it is our responsibility to prioritize the adoption of sustainable practices to safeguard the future of the Caspian Sea and its invaluable resources.

Economic significance and challenges in the fisheries sector

The Caspian Sea, a unique and diverse body of water, holds immense economic significance in various sectors, including fisheries. As politicians and diplomats, it is crucial to understand the economic potential and challenges within the fisheries sector in order to make informed decisions and policies that promote sustainable growth and development.

The fisheries industry in the Caspian Sea has historically played a significant role in the region's economy. The sea provides a rich and diverse ecosystem, supporting a wide range of fish species, including sturgeon, caviar, and various commercial fish species. The value of the Caspian Sea's fisheries is not limited to the local market; it also contributes to international trade, with exports of fish and caviar reaching global markets.

However, the fisheries sector in the Caspian Sea faces numerous challenges that must be addressed to ensure its long-term sustainability. Overfishing, illegal fishing, and the decline of certain fish populations, such as sturgeon, pose significant threats to the ecosystem and the economic viability of the sector. These challenges require collaborative efforts between countries bordering the Caspian Sea to implement effective management and conservation strategies.

Sustainable fisheries management practices, such as the establishment of protected areas, quotas, and monitoring systems, are essential for preserving fish populations and ensuring the long-term economic benefits of the sector. Additionally, promoting responsible fishing practices, raising awareness about the importance of conservation, and supporting research and scientific studies are crucial steps towards sustainable fisheries in the Caspian Sea.

Investing in the development of aquaculture and fish farming technologies is another avenue to supplement wild fish populations and reduce the pressure on natural resources. By promoting aquaculture, countries in the region can not only meet the growing demand for fish but also create employment opportunities and stimulate economic growth in coastal communities.

Furthermore, addressing environmental challenges, such as pollution and habitat degradation, is vital for the sustainability of the fisheries sector. Collaborative efforts between governments, international organizations, and stakeholders are needed to implement effective pollution control measures and promote the conservation of the Caspian Sea's biodiversity.

In conclusion, the fisheries sector in the Caspian Sea holds significant economic potential, but it also faces numerous challenges. As politicians and diplomats, it is crucial to recognize the importance of sustainable fisheries management, conservation efforts, and responsible fishing practices. By addressing these challenges collectively, we can ensure the long-term economic viability of the fisheries sector in the Caspian Sea while preserving its unique ecosystem for future generations.

Chapter 8: Tourism and Recreation Opportunities in the Caspian Sea Region

Potential for tourism development in the Caspian Sea region

The Caspian Sea region, with its unique geographical features, diverse cultures, and rich history, holds immense potential for tourism development. This subchapter explores the various opportunities and challenges in harnessing this potential, with a focus on attracting international tourists and generating economic growth in the region.

Tourism in the Caspian Sea region offers a multitude of attractions for visitors. The region boasts stunning natural landscapes, including picturesque coastlines, lush forests, and snow-capped mountains. These natural wonders provide ample opportunities for outdoor activities such as hiking, fishing, and wildlife spotting, which can be marketed to adventure-seeking tourists.

Furthermore, the Caspian Sea region is known for its cultural heritage and archaeological significance. The ancient cities along its shores, such as Baku, Astara, and Aktau, are home to historical sites, museums, and traditional markets that can be promoted to history enthusiasts and cultural tourists. The region's diverse ethnic groups and their vibrant traditions, music, and cuisine offer a unique cultural experience for visitors.

To fully exploit the tourism potential, governments in the Caspian Sea region must invest in infrastructure development and marketing campaigns. Improved transportation links, including airports, roads, and railways, will facilitate easy access for tourists. Additionally, the promotion of the region's attractions through online platforms, travel agencies, and international events will help raise awareness and attract a larger number of tourists.

However, this subchapter also highlights the need for sustainable tourism practices in the Caspian Sea region. Environmental conservation efforts should be integrated into tourism development plans to protect the fragile ecosystems and biodiversity of the region. Governments should enforce regulations and encourage eco-friendly practices among tourism operators to minimize the negative impact on the environment.

Furthermore, collaboration among Caspian Sea countries is crucial for developing cross-border touristic routes and joint marketing initiatives. This will not only enhance the tourist experience but also foster regional cooperation and stability.

In conclusion, the Caspian Sea region holds great potential for tourism development. By capitalizing on its natural beauty, cultural heritage, and archaeological significance, the region can attract international tourists and boost economic growth. However, sustainable practices and regional cooperation are essential to ensure the long-term success of tourism in the Caspian Sea region.

Cultural and natural attractions for tourists

The Caspian Sea region is not only a strategic and economic hub but also a treasure trove of cultural and natural attractions for tourists. With its rich history, diverse landscapes, and unique cultural heritage, the region offers an array of experiences that are sure to captivate travelers from all over the world.

One of the highlights of the Caspian Sea region is its cultural heritage and archaeological significance. From ancient civilizations to medieval fortresses, the region is dotted with historical sites that tell the story of its past. Tourists can explore the ruins of ancient cities such as Gorgan and Merv, marvel at the intricate architecture of the Gonbad-e Qabus

Tower, or visit the UNESCO World Heritage site of Sheki Khan's Palace in Azerbaijan.

In addition to its cultural treasures, the Caspian Sea region boasts stunning natural landscapes that are a paradise for nature lovers. The region is home to diverse ecosystems, including lush forests, vast deserts, and picturesque mountains. Tourists can go hiking in the majestic Talysh Mountains, explore the otherworldly landscapes of the Gobustan National Park, or relax on the pristine beaches of the Caspian Sea.

For those interested in marine life, the Caspian Sea offers unique opportunities for observing and interacting with its diverse aquatic species. The sea is home to a wide variety of fish species, including the famous Caspian sturgeon, which is known for its caviar. Tourists can go on fishing expeditions, visit fish farms, or even participate in sturgeon conservation projects.

Furthermore, the Caspian Sea region is a haven for adventure seekers and outdoor enthusiasts. From water sports such as sailing and windsurfing to hiking, camping, and wildlife watching, there are endless opportunities for recreation and adventure. Tourists can explore the stunning landscapes of the Khazar National Park, go birdwatching in the Saryarka – Steppe and Lakes of Northern Kazakhstan World Heritage site, or take a boat trip to the enchanting islands of the Caspian Sea.

In conclusion, the Caspian Sea region offers a wealth of cultural and natural attractions for tourists. From its rich history and archaeological sites to its stunning landscapes and diverse marine life, the region has something to offer every traveler. By promoting and preserving these attractions, policymakers can unlock the full potential of the Caspian Sea region as a tourist destination, contributing to its economic growth and development.

Sustainable tourism practices and community involvement

Sustainable tourism practices and community involvement play a vital role in the development and preservation of the Caspian Sea region. As politicians and diplomats, it is essential to understand the strategic and economic importance of adopting sustainable tourism practices and engaging local communities in order to ensure the long-term viability of the region.

One of the key benefits of sustainable tourism practices is the promotion of environmental sustainability and conservation efforts in the Caspian Sea. By implementing eco-friendly measures, such as waste management systems, renewable energy sources, and water conservation initiatives, the negative impact on the delicate ecosystem can be minimized. This not only preserves the natural beauty and biodiversity of the region but also ensures the sustainability of the tourism industry itself.

Moreover, community involvement is crucial in the development of sustainable tourism. Engaging local communities in decision-making processes and providing them with economic opportunities can help alleviate poverty and reduce dependence on unsustainable practices. This can be achieved through initiatives such as community-based tourism, where local communities actively participate in the planning and management of tourism activities and benefit directly from the revenue generated.

In addition to environmental and socio-economic benefits, sustainable tourism practices can also contribute to the cultural heritage and archaeological significance of the Caspian Sea. By promoting responsible tourism, visitors can gain a deeper understanding and appreciation of the rich cultural heritage of the region, including ancient archaeological sites and traditional customs. This not only preserves the cultural identity of local communities but also enhances the overall visitor experience.

Furthermore, sustainable tourism practices can contribute to the strategic and economic importance of the Caspian Sea as a transportation hub and trade route. By attracting tourists, the region can benefit from increased demand for transportation services, accommodation, and local products. This can stimulate economic growth, create employment opportunities, and strengthen regional integration.

In conclusion, sustainable tourism practices and community involvement are crucial in ensuring the long-term viability and success of the Caspian Sea region. By adopting eco-friendly measures, engaging local communities, and promoting responsible tourism, we can preserve the environment, enhance socio-economic development, and celebrate the cultural heritage of the region. As politicians and diplomats, it is our responsibility to champion these practices and drive the sustainable development of the Caspian Sea region for the benefit of all stakeholders.

Chapter 9: Caspian Sea as a Source of Renewable Energy, such as Wind and Tidal Power

Renewable energy potential in the Caspian Sea

The Caspian Sea is not only a significant geopolitical and economic region, but it also holds immense potential as a source of renewable energy. As politicians and diplomats, it is crucial to explore and harness this potential to promote sustainable development and reduce dependence on fossil fuels. This subchapter explores the various renewable energy sources in the Caspian Sea and their implications for the region's strategic and economic importance.

One of the most promising sources of renewable energy in the Caspian Sea is wind power. The region experiences strong and consistent winds, particularly along the coastlines, making it ideal for wind farm installations. Harnessing the power of the wind could not only provide clean and sustainable electricity but also create new job opportunities and boost the local economy. Additionally, wind power can contribute to reducing greenhouse gas emissions and combatting climate change, aligning with global sustainability goals.

Another potential source of renewable energy in the Caspian Sea is tidal power. The Caspian Sea has significant tidal movements, primarily driven by the gravitational forces of the moon and sun. By strategically placing underwater turbines in areas with strong tidal currents, it is possible to generate electricity from this renewable source. Tidal power offers a predictable and reliable energy supply, making it an attractive option for the region's energy needs.

Furthermore, the Caspian Sea has great potential for solar energy generation. With abundant sunshine throughout the year, solar panels can be installed on land and floating platforms to harness the sun's energy. Solar power can be utilized for both electricity generation and heating purposes, providing a sustainable and cost-effective solution for the region.

By tapping into the Caspian Sea's renewable energy potential, countries in the region can diversify their energy mix, reduce carbon emissions, and enhance energy security. Moreover, investing in renewable energy infrastructure can attract foreign investment, stimulate economic growth, and foster regional cooperation.

As politicians and diplomats, it is crucial to recognize the importance of renewable energy in the Caspian Sea and promote policies and initiatives that support its development. Collaboration between governments, private sector entities, and international organizations is key to unlocking the full potential of renewable energy sources in the Caspian Sea and ensuring a sustainable future for the region.

Wind power projects and initiatives

Wind power projects and initiatives in the Caspian Sea region have gained significant momentum in recent years, as countries recognize the potential of this renewable energy source to diversify their energy mix and reduce reliance on fossil fuels. Politicians and diplomats play a crucial role in shaping policies and promoting initiatives that encourage the development of wind power in the region.

The Caspian Sea, with its vast expanse and favorable wind conditions, offers an ideal setting for wind power projects. Several countries bordering the Caspian Sea, including Kazakhstan, Azerbaijan, and Turkmenistan, have already made significant investments in wind power infrastructure. These initiatives aim to harness the strong winds that sweep across the sea, converting them into clean and sustainable energy.

One notable project in the region is the Bautino Wind Power Plant in Kazakhstan, which is set to become the largest onshore wind farm in Central Asia. With a planned capacity of 50 megawatts, the project will contribute significantly to the country's goal of increasing the share of renewables in its energy mix. Similarly, Azerbaijan is making strides in wind power development, with the recently inaugurated 50-megawatt Gobustan Wind Farm being the largest in the country.

These wind power projects not only provide clean energy but also offer economic benefits. They create jobs, attract foreign investments, and stimulate local industries. Furthermore, the development of wind power in the Caspian Sea region can enhance energy security by reducing dependence on imported fossil fuels and mitigating the impact of volatile global energy markets.

To fully realize the potential of wind power in the Caspian Sea region, cross-border collaboration and cooperation are crucial. Politicians and diplomats can facilitate dialogue and partnerships between countries, encouraging the sharing of best practices, technology transfer, and joint research and development initiatives. Additionally, they can advocate for supportive regulatory frameworks and policies that promote wind power investments, such as feed-in tariffs and tax incentives.

In conclusion, wind power projects and initiatives in the Caspian Sea region hold immense strategic and economic importance. Politicians and diplomats have a critical role to play in fostering collaboration, shaping policies, and promoting investments in this renewable energy source. By harnessing the power of the wind, countries in the Caspian Sea region can achieve their energy goals, reduce greenhouse gas emissions, and contribute to a sustainable and resilient future.

Tidal power generation and future prospects

The Caspian Sea, with its vast potential and strategic importance, offers a unique opportunity for harnessing renewable energy sources, such as tidal power. Tidal power generation is a promising field that holds immense potential for the future of energy production, making it a topic of great importance for politicians and diplomats.

Tidal power is generated by the natural ebb and flow of tides caused by the gravitational pull of the moon and the sun. The Caspian Sea, with its large size and significant tidal range, is an ideal location for harnessing this renewable energy source. With its strong tidal currents, the Caspian Sea could provide a substantial amount of clean and sustainable energy.

One of the main advantages of tidal power generation is its predictability and reliability. Unlike other renewable energy sources, such as wind or solar power, tidal power can be accurately forecasted years in advance. This predictability makes it easier to integrate tidal power into the existing energy grid and ensure a stable and consistent power supply.

Furthermore, tidal power generation has minimal environmental impact compared to traditional energy sources like fossil fuels. It does not produce greenhouse gas emissions or contribute to climate change. By investing in tidal power, the Caspian Sea region can reduce its dependence on fossil fuels and move towards a more sustainable energy future.

In terms of future prospects, the development of tidal power generation in the Caspian Sea could bring numerous economic benefits. It would create job opportunities, attract investments, and stimulate economic growth in the region. Additionally, it would enhance energy security by diversifying the energy mix and reducing reliance on imported fuels.

However, there are challenges that need to be addressed for the successful implementation of tidal power generation. These include technological advancements, infrastructure development, and regulatory frameworks. Cooperation among the Caspian Sea countries is crucial to overcome these challenges and maximize the potential of tidal power.

In conclusion, tidal power generation holds significant promise for the future of energy production in the Caspian Sea region. Its predictability, minimal environmental impact, and economic benefits make it an attractive option for politicians and diplomats. By investing in tidal power, the Caspian Sea countries can secure a sustainable energy future, reduce greenhouse gas emissions, and stimulate economic growth. It is essential to prioritize the development of tidal power generation and foster regional cooperation to fully exploit the potential of this renewable energy source in the Caspian Sea.

Chapter 10: Caspian Sea as a Strategic Military and Defense Zone

Military presence and strategic importance of the Caspian Sea

The Caspian Sea is not only of great economic significance but also holds immense strategic importance in terms of military presence. This subchapter aims to shed light on the critical role the Caspian Sea plays in regional security and defense, addressing an audience of politicians and diplomats who are invested in understanding the geopolitical dynamics in the region.

The Caspian Sea region has witnessed a growing military presence over the years, with littoral states recognizing the need to protect their interests and ensure stability in the area. Each country bordering the Caspian Sea has its own security concerns, ranging from territorial disputes to potential threats from non-state actors. As a result, governments have established naval bases and deployed military assets to safeguard their national security.

The strategic importance of the Caspian Sea lies in its geographical location, which offers access to vast energy resources and key transportation routes. The sea serves as a vital link between Europe, Central Asia, and the Middle East, making it a critical transit corridor for oil and gas pipelines. Any disruption in the region can have significant consequences for global energy markets, making it imperative to maintain stability and security.

Furthermore, the Caspian Sea's proximity to conflict zones, such as the Caucasus and the Middle East, adds to its strategic significance. The region has witnessed various conflicts and security challenges in recent years, making it crucial for political leaders and diplomats to understand and address these issues effectively. Cooperation among littoral states and international partners is paramount to combatting common security threats, such as terrorism, piracy, and illicit trafficking.

In light of the increasing military presence, it is essential to promote transparency and confidence-building measures. Regular dialogues, joint military exercises, and information sharing can foster trust and cooperation among the littoral states. Additionally, diplomatic efforts should be made to resolve any existing territorial disputes and establish clear boundaries, reducing the potential for conflicts.

As politicians and diplomats, it is crucial to recognize the significance of the Caspian Sea as a strategic military and defense zone. By understanding the complexities of the region and promoting cooperation, the Caspian Sea can be safeguarded, ensuring stability, peace, and economic prosperity for the littoral states and the wider international community.

Naval capabilities and security challenges

Naval capabilities and security challenges are of utmost importance when considering the strategic and economic significance of the Caspian Sea. As politicians and diplomats, it is crucial to understand the role that naval capabilities play in ensuring the security and stability of this region.

The Caspian Sea holds immense importance due to its rich reserves of oil and gas. As such, it is vital to protect these valuable resources from any potential threats. Naval capabilities provide the necessary means to safeguard offshore oil and gas exploration and production activities, as well as the transportation routes that enable the export of these resources.

Maritime security and geopolitics in the Caspian Sea region are closely intertwined. The presence of naval forces helps deter any potential acts of aggression, piracy, or terrorism. It also allows for effective border control and surveillance, ensuring that the Caspian Sea remains a safe and secure environment for all stakeholders involved.

Environmental sustainability and conservation efforts in the Caspian Sea are also crucial. Naval capabilities can contribute to the prevention and mitigation of environmental disasters, such as oil spills, by enabling rapid response and containment measures. Additionally, they can support efforts to combat illegal fishing and protect marine biodiversity, ensuring the long-term viability of the Caspian Sea's ecosystem.

Moreover, the Caspian Sea's potential as a transportation hub and trade route depends on a secure maritime environment. Naval capabilities provide protection for commercial vessels, facilitating the movement of goods and boosting regional trade. They also contribute to the establishment of international maritime laws and regulations, ensuring fair and efficient maritime commerce.

The Caspian Sea's strategic military and defense zone status cannot be overlooked. Naval capabilities are essential for maintaining a robust defense posture and deterring potential threats. They enable effective monitoring and control of the Caspian Sea's waters, safeguarding the sovereignty and territorial integrity of the littoral states.

Finally, the cultural heritage, archaeological significance, and rare mineral and resource potential of the Caspian Sea must be protected. Naval capabilities can play a vital role in preserving and studying the region's cultural heritage and archaeological sites. Additionally, they can support scientific research and exploration to harness the Caspian Sea's rare minerals and resources sustainably.

In conclusion, naval capabilities are crucial for addressing the security challenges faced in the Caspian Sea region. They contribute to the protection of oil and gas exploration, maritime security, environmental sustainability, trade, defense, cultural heritage, and resource exploitation.

As politicians and diplomats, it is essential to recognize the significance of naval capabilities in maintaining the strategic and economic importance of the Caspian Sea.

Cooperation and confidence-building measures among littoral states

In the complex geopolitical landscape of the Caspian Sea, cooperation and confidence-building measures among the littoral states play a crucial role in ensuring stability, security, and sustainable development in the region. This subchapter explores the significance of fostering cooperation and trust among these states, highlighting the potential benefits and challenges they face.

For politicians and diplomats, understanding the strategic and economic importance of the Caspian Sea is essential. The region is rich in oil and gas reserves, making it a key player in global energy markets. Cooperation among littoral states in the exploration and production of these resources can lead to increased energy security and economic prosperity for all parties involved.

Maritime security and geopolitics are also paramount concerns in the Caspian Sea region. Cooperation in sharing information, intelligence, and resources is crucial to combatting piracy, terrorism, and other security threats. Confidence-building measures, such as joint military exercises and intelligence sharing, can contribute to a more secure and stable maritime environment.

Environmental sustainability and conservation efforts are of growing importance in the Caspian Sea. Cooperation among littoral states in addressing pollution, overfishing, and habitat degradation is vital to protect the delicate ecosystem and preserve biodiversity. By sharing best practices and collaborating on conservation initiatives, the states can work towards a sustainable future for the Caspian Sea.

Furthermore, the Caspian Sea has the potential to serve as a transportation hub and trade route, linking Europe, Asia, and the Middle East. Cooperation among littoral states in developing efficient and secure transport infrastructure can enhance regional connectivity and economic integration.

The Caspian Sea is not only a source of fossil fuels but also renewable energy such as wind and tidal power. Collaborative efforts in harnessing these resources can contribute to a greener energy mix and reduce dependence on traditional energy sources.

In addition, the Caspian Sea holds cultural heritage and archaeological significance, which can be explored through joint research and preservation projects. The sea also offers rare minerals and resources that can be sustainably exploited through cooperation among littoral states.

In conclusion, cooperation and confidence-building measures among the littoral states of the Caspian Sea are essential for addressing various challenges and harnessing the region's vast potential. By working together, politicians and diplomats can foster stability, security, and sustainable development across the niches of strategic importance, economic prosperity, maritime security, environmental sustainability, transportation, cultural heritage, and rare resources.

Chapter 11: Cultural Heritage and Archaeological Significance of the Caspian Sea

Historical and archaeological sites in the Caspian Sea region

The Caspian Sea region is not only rich in natural resources and strategic importance but also boasts a wealth of historical and archaeological sites that hold significant cultural and scientific value. These sites provide a glimpse into the region's past and offer a unique opportunity to understand the historical and cultural development of the Caspian Sea region. In this subchapter, we will explore some of the notable historical and archaeological sites in the Caspian Sea region.

One such site is the ancient city of Baku, located on the western coast of the Caspian Sea. Baku has a rich history dating back thousands of years and is known for its well-preserved medieval architecture and the UNESCO World Heritage-listed Old City. The Old City, or Icheri Sheher, is home to the iconic Maiden Tower and the Palace of the Shirvanshahs, both of which serve as reminders of the region's ancient past.

Another important archaeological site in the Caspian Sea region is Gobustan, located on the southeastern coast of the sea. Gobustan is renowned for its rock art, which dates back to the Upper Paleolithic era. These rock carvings depict various scenes of hunting, dancing, and daily life, providing valuable insights into the region's prehistoric cultures.

Further along the coast, the city of Derbent stands as one of the oldest continually inhabited cities in the world. With a history dating back over 5,000 years, Derbent has witnessed the rise and fall of numerous empires and is home to ancient fortifications, including the UNESCO World Heritage-listed Naryn-Kala fortress.

The Caspian Sea region is also home to the ancient city of Merv, located in present-day Turkmenistan. Merv was a major center of trade and culture along the Silk Road and served as the capital of several empires throughout history. The archaeological site of Merv contains the ruins of ancient palaces, mausoleums, and mosques, showcasing the region's rich architectural heritage.

These historical and archaeological sites in the Caspian Sea region not only hold cultural significance but also have the potential to boost tourism and recreation opportunities. By preserving and promoting these sites, policymakers can create a sustainable tourism industry that contributes to the region's economic development. Moreover, these sites serve as a testament to the historical and cultural diversity of the Caspian Sea region, fostering greater appreciation and understanding among its inhabitants and visitors alike.

Preservation and promotion of cultural heritage

The Caspian Sea region is not only known for its strategic and economic importance, but it also holds a rich cultural heritage that deserves preservation and promotion. As politicians and diplomats, it is crucial to recognize the significance of cultural heritage in fostering understanding, cooperation, and sustainable development among nations.

The Caspian Sea region has been a melting pot of diverse cultures, civilizations, and historical influences for centuries. From the ancient Silk Road to the medieval Islamic empires, the region has witnessed the rise and fall of numerous civilizations, leaving behind a treasure trove of archaeological sites, monuments, and artifacts.

Preserving and promoting the cultural heritage of the Caspian Sea region can have several benefits. Firstly, it can strengthen the sense of identity and pride among the local populations, fostering a shared sense of belonging and unity. This, in turn, can contribute to social cohesion and stability in the region.

Secondly, the cultural heritage of the Caspian Sea region has immense potential for tourism and recreation opportunities. By showcasing the historical sites, museums, and cultural events, the region can attract both domestic and international tourists, boosting the local economy and creating job opportunities.

Moreover, the preservation of cultural heritage can serve as a basis for educational and research activities. Universities and research institutions can collaborate with local communities to study and document the historical and archaeological significance of the region. This can lead to a better understanding of the past and provide insights into the development of civilizations.

To ensure the preservation and promotion of cultural heritage in the Caspian Sea region, it is essential to establish effective conservation mechanisms. This includes developing comprehensive legal frameworks, establishing dedicated cultural heritage institutions, and providing financial resources for restoration and maintenance efforts.

Furthermore, international cooperation and collaboration among the Caspian Sea countries are crucial in this endeavor. Sharing best practices, expertise, and resources can enhance the preservation efforts and promote cultural exchange among nations.

In conclusion, the Caspian Sea region's cultural heritage is a valuable asset that should be protected, preserved, and promoted. By recognizing its significance, politicians and diplomats can contribute to fostering understanding, cooperation, and sustainable development in the region. Through effective conservation measures and international collaboration, the cultural heritage of the Caspian Sea can be safeguarded for future generations to appreciate and learn from.

Importance of cultural diplomacy in the Caspian Sea region

Cultural diplomacy plays a crucial role in fostering understanding, building trust, and promoting cooperation among nations. In the unique context of the Caspian Sea region, where diverse cultures and civilizations converge, the importance of cultural diplomacy cannot be overstated. This subchapter explores the significance of cultural diplomacy in the Caspian Sea region, highlighting its potential to strengthen relationships between nations, enhance economic cooperation, and preserve the rich cultural heritage of the region.

Cultural diplomacy acts as a bridge between nations, enabling politicians and diplomats to engage in constructive dialogue and develop mutual understanding. In a region as geopolitically complex as the Caspian Sea, cultural diplomacy can play a vital role in mitigating tensions and fostering a climate of collaboration. By promoting cultural exchanges, joint artistic endeavors, and educational programs, cultural diplomacy can build trust and facilitate diplomatic negotiations.

Moreover, cultural diplomacy has immense economic potential in the Caspian Sea region. As oil and gas exploration and production form a significant part of the region's economy, cultural diplomacy can help establish partnerships and attract foreign investment. By showcasing the unique cultural assets of each country, cultural diplomacy can create a favorable environment for business collaborations and economic growth.

Preserving and promoting the rich cultural heritage of the Caspian Sea region is another crucial aspect of cultural diplomacy. The region boasts a wealth of archaeological sites, historical landmarks, and traditional arts and crafts. Through cultural diplomacy initiatives, politicians and diplomats can work together to protect and showcase these treasures, fostering a sense of pride and identity among the local communities.

Furthermore, cultural diplomacy can contribute to environmental sustainability and conservation efforts in the Caspian Sea. By promoting cultural practices that prioritize the preservation of natural resources, politicians and diplomats can encourage responsible fishing, aquaculture, and tourism practices. This can help maintain the ecological balance of the sea and ensure its long-term viability as a source of renewable energy and rare minerals.

In conclusion, cultural diplomacy plays a pivotal role in the Caspian Sea region, addressing the diverse niches of strategic and economic importance, oil and gas exploration, maritime security, environmental sustainability, transportation, fisheries, tourism, renewable energy, military defense, cultural heritage, and rare resources. By fostering understanding, promoting economic cooperation, preserving cultural heritage, and contributing to environmental sustainability, cultural diplomacy serves as a powerful tool for politicians and diplomats to navigate the complexities and unlock the vast potential of the Caspian Sea region.

Chapter 12: Caspian Sea as a Source of Rare Minerals and Resources

Mineral resources and potential extraction in the Caspian Sea

The Caspian Sea, with its immense size and unique geographical position, holds significant potential for mineral resources and extraction. This subchapter explores the diverse range of minerals found in the Caspian Sea and the potential economic benefits they offer.

Underneath the seabed lies an abundance of oil and gas reserves, making the Caspian Sea a crucial region for the oil and gas industry. The discovery of these reserves has attracted international attention and investment, leading to the establishment of numerous exploration and production projects. As politicians and diplomats, it is important to recognize the strategic and economic significance of these resources and ensure their sustainable extraction for the benefit of all Caspian Sea nations.

In addition to oil and gas, the Caspian Sea is also rich in other minerals such as sulfur, salt, and limestone. These resources have a wide range of applications, including industrial use, agriculture, and construction. By tapping into these resources, the Caspian Sea region can enhance its economic growth and development.

However, it is essential to approach mineral extraction in the Caspian Sea with caution and consideration for environmental sustainability. The delicate ecosystem of the sea, home to numerous species of flora and fauna, must be protected. Efforts should be made to minimize the impact of extraction activities and establish conservation measures to preserve the biodiversity of the region.

Furthermore, the Caspian Sea can serve as a potential source of renewable energy, such as wind and tidal power. The strong winds and currents in the region make it ideal for harnessing these forms of energy. Developing renewable energy projects not only helps diversify the energy mix but also contributes to the reduction of greenhouse gas emissions.

As a strategic military and defense zone, the Caspian Sea plays a vital role in ensuring regional security. The presence of mineral resources in the sea adds to its strategic importance, making it imperative for politicians and diplomats to address the geopolitical challenges and promote cooperation among Caspian Sea nations.

In conclusion, the Caspian Sea offers significant opportunities for mineral extraction, including oil and gas reserves, as well as other minerals. Careful consideration must be given to environmental sustainability, ensuring the preservation of the sea's biodiversity. Additionally, the Caspian Sea can serve as a source of renewable energy and contribute to regional security. By recognizing and harnessing the potential of the sea's mineral resources, politicians and diplomats can promote economic growth, sustainable development, and cooperation among the Caspian Sea nations.

Environmental and economic considerations

The Caspian Sea, often referred to as a "sea of opportunities," possesses immense strategic and economic importance. As politicians and diplomats, it is crucial to understand the environmental and economic considerations associated with this unique body of water.

One of the primary concerns is the impact of oil and gas exploration and production in the Caspian Sea. The region is known for its vast energy reserves, attracting major multinational companies. However, stringent regulations and sustainable practices must be implemented to minimize environmental degradation and ensure long-term economic benefits.

Maritime security and geopolitics in the Caspian Sea region are other crucial aspects to consider. The sea serves as a vital trade route connecting Central Asia, the Caucasus, and Europe. Cooperation among nations is essential to maintain stability, combat piracy, and address territorial disputes, thereby safeguarding economic interests.

Environmental sustainability and conservation efforts in the Caspian Sea are of utmost importance. The delicate marine ecosystem supports a diverse range of flora and fauna, including endangered species. Implementing conservation measures, such as regulating fishing practices and reducing pollution, will contribute to the long-term preservation of this unique environment.

Moreover, the Caspian Sea's potential as a transportation hub and trade route cannot be overlooked. Investments in infrastructure, such as ports and shipping facilities, will enhance connectivity within the region and open up new economic opportunities.

The Caspian Sea also holds immense potential as a source of renewable energy, such as wind and tidal power. Utilizing these resources can reduce reliance on fossil fuels and contribute to global efforts to combat climate change.

Additionally, the Caspian Sea's strategic military and defense zone status is significant. Cooperation among nations in terms of security and defense will ensure stability in the region and protect economic interests.

The cultural heritage and archaeological significance of the Caspian Sea further contribute to its overall value. Preserving and promoting this rich heritage will attract tourists and boost the local economy while fostering a sense of pride and identity among the local population.

Lastly, the Caspian Sea's abundance of rare minerals and resources presents economic opportunities for sustainable extraction and utilization. Responsible resource management can provide significant economic benefits while minimizing environmental impact.

In conclusion, the Caspian Sea is a complex ecosystem with immense strategic and economic value. By addressing environmental sustainability, promoting responsible resource management, and enhancing maritime security, politicians and diplomats can ensure the long-term prosperity of the region while protecting its unique natural and cultural heritage.

Sustainable resource management and international cooperation

Sustainable resource management and international cooperation is a crucial aspect when it comes to harnessing the strategic and economic importance of the Caspian Sea. As politicians and diplomats, it is essential to understand the significance of sustainable practices in order to ensure the long-term viability of the region's resources.

The Caspian Sea is known for its vast reserves of oil and gas, making it a prime location for exploration and production. However, in order to mitigate the environmental impact and ensure the sustainability of these resources, international cooperation is needed. Collaboration between countries bordering the Caspian Sea is necessary to establish regulations and guidelines for responsible extraction and production practices. This includes measures to prevent oil spills, minimize pollution, and protect marine life.

In addition to oil and gas, the Caspian Sea also holds immense potential as a renewable energy source. Wind and tidal power can be harnessed to provide clean and sustainable energy for the region. International cooperation is crucial for the development of renewable energy infrastructure, sharing of technological advancements, and establishing frameworks for the sustainable utilization of these resources.

Another important aspect of sustainable resource management is the conservation of the Caspian Sea's biodiversity. The region is home to a diverse range of marine species, and the preservation of their habitats is crucial for maintaining ecological balance. International cooperation can facilitate the establishment of protected areas, the enforcement of fishing regulations, and the promotion of sustainable aquaculture practices.

International cooperation is also vital in addressing maritime security and geopolitical challenges in the Caspian Sea region. Cooperation between countries can help combat piracy, smuggling, and illegal fishing activities. Collaborative efforts can also address territorial disputes and ensure the peaceful and stable development of the region.

Furthermore, the Caspian Sea's potential as a transportation hub and trade route can be maximized through international cooperation. Developing efficient and sustainable transportation infrastructure can facilitate the movement of goods and promote economic growth in the region. Cooperation in this area can involve the harmonization of customs procedures, the development of multimodal transport networks, and the establishment of trade agreements.

Lastly, the Caspian Sea is not only a source of economic and strategic importance but also holds significant cultural and archaeological heritage. International cooperation is crucial in preserving and promoting this heritage through the protection of archaeological sites, the establishment of cultural tourism initiatives, and the exchange of knowledge and expertise.

In conclusion, sustainable resource management and international cooperation are vital aspects in harnessing the strategic and economic importance of the Caspian Sea. Through collaboration, politicians and diplomats can work together to ensure responsible extraction and production practices, promote renewable energy sources, conserve biodiversity, address maritime security challenges, develop efficient transportation networks, protect cultural heritage, and maximize the region's potential for sustainable development.

Chapter 13: Conclusion and Recommendations

Summary of key findings and insights

The book "Navigating the Caspian: The Strategic and Economic Importance of the Sea" provides a comprehensive analysis of various aspects related to the Caspian Sea. Targeted towards politicians and diplomats, this subchapter aims to summarize key findings and insights of the book that are relevant to their interests.

The Caspian Sea holds immense strategic and economic importance. One key finding is that the sea is a rich source of oil and gas reserves, making it a crucial region for exploration and production. The book explores the potential for further development in this sector, highlighting the opportunities and challenges associated with it.

Maritime security and geopolitics in the Caspian Sea region is another significant topic discussed in the book. It emphasizes the need for cooperative efforts among the littoral states to address security concerns and promote stability in the region. The insights provided offer valuable guidance for politicians and diplomats involved in regional security discussions.

Environmental sustainability and conservation efforts in the Caspian Sea are also highlighted. The book underscores the importance of protecting the sea's unique ecosystem and biodiversity. It presents findings related to environmental challenges, such as pollution and overfishing, and offers insights into conservation strategies that can be pursued.

Furthermore, the Caspian Sea presents significant opportunities as a transportation hub and trade route. The book explores the potential for enhanced connectivity and trade partnerships among the littoral states, highlighting the economic benefits that can be derived from improved transportation infrastructure.

Other key findings and insights include the potential for fisheries and aquaculture development, tourism and recreation opportunities, and the Caspian Sea as a source of renewable energy. Additionally, the book delves into the strategic military and defense significance of the Caspian Sea, as well as its cultural heritage, archaeological significance, and its potential as a source of rare minerals and resources.

Overall, this subchapter provides a concise summary of the book's key findings and insights, offering politicians and diplomats a comprehensive understanding of the strategic and economic importance of the Caspian Sea. It equips them with valuable knowledge to make informed decisions and engage in meaningful discussions related to the region's development and cooperation.

Policy recommendations for politicians and diplomats

The Caspian Sea holds immense strategic and economic importance, making it crucial for politicians and diplomats to prioritize effective policies. This subchapter aims to provide recommendations that address the various niches related to the Caspian Sea, catering specifically to the audience of politicians and diplomats.

1. The Strategic and Economic Importance of the Caspian Sea:

a. Foster regional cooperation and dialogue to promote stability and enhance economic integration among the Caspian littoral states.

b. Support the development of a comprehensive legal framework to govern maritime boundaries, resource allocation, and transportation infrastructure.

2. Oil and Gas Exploration and Production in the Caspian Sea:

a. Encourage sustainable development practices and responsible extraction techniques to protect the environment and prevent ecological damage.

b. Facilitate the establishment of a transparent and fair regulatory framework that ensures equitable distribution of oil and gas revenues among the littoral states.

3. Maritime Security and Geopolitics in the Caspian Sea Region:

a. Enhance cooperation among littoral states to combat piracy, terrorism, and other transnational organized crimes.

b. Promote confidence-building measures, such as joint maritime patrols and information sharing, to reduce tensions and enhance regional security.

4. Environmental Sustainability and Conservation Efforts in the Caspian Sea:

a. Invest in research and development to better understand the Caspian Sea's ecosystem and its vulnerability to climate change.

b. Promote conservation initiatives, including the creation of marine protected areas, to preserve biodiversity and sustainably manage natural resources.

5. Caspian Sea as a Transportation Hub and Trade Route:

a. Improve transportation infrastructure, such as ports, railways, and roads, to enhance connectivity and facilitate trade within the region.

b. Facilitate the harmonization of customs procedures and regulations to reduce trade barriers and promote cross-border economic integration.

6. Fisheries and Aquaculture in the Caspian Sea:

a. Implement sustainable fishing practices and regulate fishing quotas to prevent overfishing and ensure the long-term viability of fish stocks.

b. Support the development of aquaculture projects to reduce pressure on wild fish populations and create new economic opportunities.

7. Tourism and Recreation Opportunities in the Caspian Sea Region:

a. Promote the unique cultural heritage and natural beauty of the Caspian Sea to attract tourists and boost local economies.

b. Invest in infrastructure and services to develop sustainable tourism practices that protect the environment and respect local communities.

8. Caspian Sea as a Source of Renewable Energy, such as Wind and Tidal Power:

a. Encourage investment in renewable energy projects, such as wind farms and tidal power plants, to diversify energy sources and reduce dependence on fossil fuels.

b. Facilitate cross-border energy cooperation and the sharing of best practices to harness the full potential of renewable energy in the Caspian Sea region.

9. Caspian Sea as a Strategic Military and Defense Zone:

a. Strengthen regional security cooperation, including joint military exercises and information sharing, to address common security challenges and promote stability.

b. Encourage dialogue and confidence-building measures to reduce tensions and prevent the escalation of conflicts in the region.

10. Cultural Heritage and Archaeological Significance of the Caspian Sea:

a. Support efforts to preserve and promote the rich cultural heritage of the Caspian Sea region through the establishment of cultural exchange programs and heritage protection initiatives.

b. Facilitate international collaboration in archaeological research and excavation to enhance our understanding of the region's history and cultural contributions.

11. Caspian Sea as a Source of Rare Minerals and Resources:

a. Encourage responsible and sustainable extraction practices to minimize environmental impact and ensure the equitable distribution of wealth among the littoral states.

b. Promote transparency and accountability in resource exploitation to prevent corruption and promote fair trade practices.

By implementing these policy recommendations, politicians and diplomats can work towards harnessing the full potential of the Caspian Sea while ensuring its long-term sustainability and stability for the benefit of the region and its people.

Future prospects and potential for the Caspian Sea region

As politicians and diplomats, it is crucial to understand the future prospects and potential of the Caspian Sea region, as it holds significant strategic and economic importance. This subchapter aims to shed light on various aspects, including the strategic and economic importance of the Caspian Sea, oil and gas exploration and production, maritime security, environmental sustainability, transportation and trade, fisheries and aquaculture, tourism and recreation opportunities, renewable energy sources, military and defense, cultural heritage, and rare minerals and resources.

The Caspian Sea region has immense strategic and economic importance due to its vast reserves of oil and gas. The exploration and production activities in this region have attracted major international companies, fostering economic growth and energy security. However, challenges such as maritime security and geopolitics need to be addressed to ensure stability and sustainable development in the region.

Environmental sustainability and conservation efforts are crucial for the Caspian Sea region. The unique ecosystem and biodiversity of the Caspian Sea are at risk due to pollution, overfishing, and habitat destruction. Collaborative efforts among countries are needed to protect and restore this valuable natural resource.

The Caspian Sea also has the potential to become a major transportation hub and trade route, connecting Europe and Asia. Developing efficient transport infrastructure and promoting international cooperation will enhance regional connectivity and boost trade relations.

Fisheries and aquaculture in the Caspian Sea offer significant economic opportunities, contributing to food security and livelihoods. Sustainable management practices and scientific research are essential to ensure the long-term viability of these resources.

The Caspian Sea region has untapped potential for tourism and recreational activities. Its unique coastal landscapes, historical sites, and cultural heritage attract both domestic and international tourists. Investments in infrastructure and promotion of sustainable tourism practices can further boost this sector.

Furthermore, the Caspian Sea holds immense potential as a source of renewable energy, such as wind and tidal power. Investing in clean energy technologies will not only reduce environmental impact but also diversify the energy mix and enhance energy security.

The Caspian Sea's strategic location makes it a crucial military and defense zone. Cooperation among littoral states is essential to ensure regional stability and prevent conflicts. Strengthening naval capabilities and sharing intelligence will enhance security in the region.

Lastly, the Caspian Sea is of great cultural and archaeological significance. Its shores are home to ancient civilizations and archaeological sites, attracting researchers and historians from around the world. Preserving and promoting this cultural heritage will contribute to the region's identity and tourism potential.

Additionally, the Caspian Sea is a potential source of rare minerals and resources, offering economic opportunities for the region. Responsible extraction and sustainable management practices will ensure the long-term benefits of these resources.

In conclusion, understanding the future prospects and potential of the Caspian Sea region is crucial for politicians and diplomats. By addressing the strategic and economic importance, oil and gas exploration, maritime security, environmental sustainability, transportation, fisheries, tourism, renewable energy, military and defense, cultural heritage, and rare minerals, the region can unlock its full potential and achieve sustainable development.

www.ingramcontent.com/pod-product-compliance
Lightning Source LLC
Chambersburg PA
CBHW051255160726
47994CB00003B/1169